On the PRACTICE of WITCHCRAFT

---

*The Malice and Mischief
of Witches, Of the Devils Mark
and Of the Grimoire*

By

MONTAGUE SUMMERS

This edition published by Read Books Ltd.
Copyright © 2019 Read Books Ltd.
This book is copyright and may not be
reproduced or copied in any way without
the express permission of the publisher in writing

British Library Cataloguing-in-Publication Data
A catalogue record for this book is available
from the British Library

"All magic, all witchcraft, depends on the Devil, and is fundamentally evil."

MONTAGUE SUMMERS

CONTENTS

Montague Summers 7
ON THE PRACTICE OF WITCHCRAFT 9

Montague Summers

Augustus Montague Summers was born in Bristol, England in 1880. He was raised as an evangelical Anglican in a wealthy family, and studied at Clifton College before reading theology at Trinity College, Oxford with the intention of becoming a Church of England priest. In 1905, he graduated with fourth-class honours, and went on to continue his religious training at the Lichfield Theological College. Summers entered his apprenticeship as a curate in the diocese of Bitton near Bristol, but rumours of an interest in Satanism and accusations of sexual misconduct with young boys led to him being cut off; a scandal which dogged him his whole life. Summers joined the growing ranks of English men of letters interested in medievalism and the occult. In 1909, he converted to Catholicism and shortly thereafter he began passing himself off as a Catholic priest, the legitimacy of which was disputed. Around this time, Summers adopted a curious attire which included a sweeping black cape and a silver-topped cane.

Summers eventually managed to make a living as a full-time writer. He was interested in the theatre of the seventeenth century, particularly that of the English Restoration, and was one of the founder members of The Phoenix, a society that performed neglected works of that era. In 1916, he was elected a fellow of the Royal Society of Literature. Summers also produced some important studies of Gothic fiction. However, his interest in the occult never waned, and in 1928, around the time he was acquainted with Aleister Crowley, he published the first English translation of Heinrich Kramer and James Sprenger's *Malleus Maleficarum* ('*The Hammer of Witches*'), a 15th century Latin text on the hunting of witches. Summers then turned to vampires, producing *The Vampire: His Kith and Kin* (1928) and

The Vampire in Europe (1929), and then to werewolves with *The Werewolf* (1933). Summers' work on the occult is known for his unusual, archaic writing style, his intimate style of narration, and his purported belief in the reality of the subjects he treats.

In his day, Summers was a renowned eccentric; *The Times* called him "*in every way a 'character'*" *and "a throwback to the Middle Ages."* He died at his home in Richmond, Surrey.

ON THE PRACTICE OF WITCHCRAFT

OF THE MALICE AND MISCHIEF OF WITCHES; OF THE DEVILS MARK; AND OF THE GRIMOIRE

Then flourish Hell, and mighty Mischief reign !
            DRYDEN, *The Duke of Guise.*
Many of them also which used curious arts brought their books together, and burned them before all men : and they counted the price of them, and found it fifty thousand pieces of silver.
            The Acts of the Apostles, xix, 19.

The most complete, as it is certainly the most authoritative, summary of the mischiefs wrought by witchcraft is that delivered in the famous Bull of Innocent VIII where the evil is set forth in words of burning eloquence and conviction : " Many persons of both sexes unmindful of their own salvation and straying from the Catholic Faith, have abandoned themselves to devils, incubi and succubi, and by their incantations, spells, conjurations, and other accursed charms and crafts, enormities and horrid offences, have slain infants yet in the mother's womb, as also the offspring of cattle, have blasted the produce of the earth, the grapes of the vine, the fruits of trees, nay, men and women, beasts of burthen, herd-beasts, as well as animals of other kinds, vineyards, orchards, meadows, pasture-land, corn, wheat, and all other cereals ; these wretches furthermore afflict and torment men and women, beasts of burthen, herd-beasts, as well as animals of other kinds, with terrible and piteous pains and sore diseases, both internal and external ;

they hinder men from performing the sexual act and women from conceiving, whence husbands cannot know their wives nor wives receive their husbands; over and above this they blasphemously renounce that Faith which is theirs by the Sacrament of Baptism, and at the instigation of the Enemy of Mankind they do not shrink from committing and perpetrating the foulest abominations and filthiest excesses to the deadly peril of their souls whereby they outrage the Divine Majesty and are a cause of scandal and danger to very many."

This historical pronouncement carries no mere historical interest. The wisdom of Pope Innocent is speaking to us to-day, and his words are as awfully solemn and as eternally true in the twentieth century as they were four hundred and more years ago. We have in these noble sentences set forth the very essence of witchcraft, that is to say the implacable hate the witch bears all mankind, and the dark power these slaves of Satan have obtained to contrive damage and destruction, ay, even of life, to the glut of their murderous malice and malignity.

The witch is an evil thing, indeed; a social pest and parasite; the devotee of a loathly and obscene creed; an adept at poisoning, blackmail, and other creeping crimes; a bawd; an abortionist; a minister to vice and corruption, battening upon the foulest passions of the age. Witches

                              raise jars,
Jealousies, strifes, and heart-burning disagreements,
Like a thick scurf o'er life.

Their baneful activities range from domestic annoyances and accidents, singly trivial enough maybe, but in sum horribly fretting and vexatious, to the most serious injuries, the ruin of property, sudden illness and wasting death, and ultimately to the embroiling of nations, to anarchy and red revolution, for the witch is and always has been a political factor. The witch is, in effect, a perpetual menace, a source of instant danger to any ordered society. In the humblest walks of life, in townlets and small villages, witches although almost isolated members of the infernal organization are yet potential murderers, even as the master whom they serve was a murderer from the beginning.

A correspondent in *The Times*, 19th September, 1930, writes : " In 1900 I was living in a small Sussex village between Groombridge and Eastbourne. An old villager one day began to talk about witches. ' The worst on 'em about here's not long dead,' she said. She told me a few of the common tales, injuring children, damaging poultry, &c. Then she warmed up. Pointing to the adjacent cross-roads, she said : ' I was standing just there, one day, and *she* was there. Along come one of Squire ———'s big farm carts, you know, him at the Park.' (Just then ' the Park ' was let to ' furriners '—i.e. non-Sussex people.) ' *She* looked at it, and down went the horses into the road over their knees, and the cart over the axles.' "

Another correspondent in the same paper, three days later, related that when he was living in a small town in Somerset about 1912–13 he used to visit an old woman who told him that she had had an ulcerated leg ever since she came to the town and that there was no hope of her getting any better, since her ailment was due to a bad woman next door who had come and overlooked her one midnight. She further remarked that Somerset was particularly full of " bad folk ", that is to say witches. I suggest that the secret tradition has been handed down from the days of Julian Cox, Ann Bishop, and Margaret Agar.

In February, 1923, at Gorefield, a small village in Cambridgeshire, Mr. Scrimshaw and his family were bewitched, and much distress ensued in the house. Mrs. Holmes, who lived about a mile away, claimed to be able to break the spell as she had been " born in Chime-hours ". I will do what I can to help neighbour Scrimshaw," she said, " if they are witching him I can stop them." She collected some apple pips; some locks of hair and nail parings from each member of the family, and these with two black pins she put in a bottle which was thrown on the kitchen fire. As the bottle burst she declared the charm was broken. However, new disturbances took place at the farm, coincident with which Mrs. Holmes died (*The Evening Standard*, 19th March, 1923).

Four peasants were tried at Szeged (Hungary) in January, 1928, for having killed an old woman, alleged to be a witch. The defendants were near relations of Vincent Tokar, who had long been bedridden owing to the malice of this hag. She visited him at night, and by her cantrips drained him dry as hay so that he dwindled, peaked and pined, and was left in so pitiable a state that his cousins resolved even with violence to free him from the evil spell. That evening they waited in the bedchamber, and when the woman entered swiftly dispatched her. The court acquitted the accused since they had acted under irresistible compulsion being compelled to believe in the stated origin of Tokar's illness. Moreover in the circumstances the case indicated the existence of a witch.

Some two years later there was a similar occurrence in a Hungarian village. A well-to-do farmer was seized with a sudden fever. One evening the sick man, raving in delirium, shouted that a witch had seized him by the throat and cast a curse upon him. " Save me from the witch," he cried, " she will appear at midnight." For three nights the family kept vigil, and on the third night as the church clock was striking twelve the door was flung open and a fearful crone hobbled in, but the men of the house sprang on her and a blow laid her dead on the floor. At that very moment the farmer rose from his bed, completely cured. Those concerned were tried for homicide and sentenced to short terms of imprisonment, which were much reduced by the Supreme Court at Vienna.

In September, 1928, Camilla Illasi was convicted at Padua of witchcraft, cruelty to animals, and extortion. She had terrorized the village of Bassanello for years, trafficking in black magic. She kept numbers of birds, dogs, cats, and rabbits which she used for her foul charms and auguries. The peasantry feared and hated the witch, who long cunningly evaded the law, but at last she was caught and reaped the full reward of her iniquities.

Writing in *The Church Times*, 8th May, 1931, and describing the Essex village of Good Easter, Donald Maxwell remarks that the people are still firmly convinced of the power of witchcraft and the evil eye. " There was no doubt whatever that old Mother Blankley was a witch. There was proof of it. What about Farmer Attridge's heifers and the strange litter of pigs in Old Mead's barn? She was a witch right enough."

A tourist in Cardiganshire writing in *The Daily Express*, 27th December, 1932, evinces surprise that in Wales to-day many people believe firmly in the power of witchcraft and the evil eye. " I was positive that my little pig was bewitched when one day he sat up on his haunches in the sty and laughed at me like a woman I know. I went to the wizard about it," one woman told him. Another woman said that when her two pigs refused to eat she consulted a wise man, who instructed her : " After sunset take a few hairs from the pigs' backs. Rub them into a ball of lard. Put the tongs over the fire and place the ball of lard on it. You must be alone. You will see a blue flame and in it the face of the person who bewitched your pigs. Feed the pigs next morning." This was done, the pigs were cured and the following day they ran to their food.

A few years ago a lady who was walking through the market square at Tavistock saw an old woman pilfering small articles from the stalls. She called the attention of one of the sellers to this, whereupon the hag swiftly turning round asked : " With which eye did you see all this ? " " With both my eyes," was the reply. The old woman muttered quickly to herself, and added aloud : " For meddling with what does not concern you, by this and that you shall see no more." So saying she waved her hand swiftly across the lady's face, not touching her, and hobbled away. Within an hour the lady lost her sight, and blind she remained until the day she died, which was in 1931.

A correspondent in *John O'London's Weekly*, November, 1936, observed that " even now belief in witchcraft in the upper parts of the Wye Valley is not quite extinct ". Mr. E. Thomas, writing in the following month, remarked, " when we lived in a small village in Montgomeryshire some years ago we found a widespread belief in witchcraft among the farmers of the district." If the cattle became sick the farmers visited the conjurer at LL—— to inquire who had bewitched their beasts. When two farmers had a serious quarrel, one of them went to the conjurer to procure a charm to injure his neighbour.

Other methods a witch might employ to plague her neighbours were by making the cows go dry, and so stealing the milk ; by enchanting the churn, whence butter would not come ; by burning the bread in the oven or souring it ; by spoiling the ale at brewing time. To us to-day generally these mishaps may not mean so much, for they can at least fairly easily be rectified, they may even appear a trifle ridiculous, not to say comical. But two centuries and less ago (and in some remoter districts now) when a household might depend for its comfort, nay, even for its sustenance, upon the success of these domestic operations things wear a very different face, and such malicious interference would have very disastrous results. Examples of all these mischiefs occur again and again throughout the witch trials. Alice Martin, a Devonshire witch, arraigned in 1565, used to enter houses begging for milk. If refused she would mutter " Give no milk : give no milk ", and from that day they could make no butter nor cheese nor have milk from their kine. About ten years ago there was a notorious witch living in

Caithness who wished to buy a young cow from a neighbouring farm. The owner refused to sell, saying he needed the milk. The witch replied that he would never again get milk from that cow, and her words came true. More recently a Welsh farmer was charged with assault. He had drawn blood from a reputed witch, and had compelled her to come to his house and unspeak the churn. He probably acted under great provocation and was justified in his somewhat rough and ready procedure.

Mother Waterhouse, one of the Chelmsford coven, who was hanged in 1566, confessed that she had sent her familiar to destroy the brewing. Mother Palmer, of Framlingham, came to Robert Waite's house and asked for a draught of beer. She was refused, and answered the goodwife, "You will want a cup o' beer yourself before long." After that they could make no beer which did not sour in a couple of weeks. The demon of Tedworth, who incited by the villainy and witchcrafts of the drummer, so plagued Mr. Mompesson's house, used to spoil the food by filling the porringers with ashes.

In Guernsey, not many years ago, a witch ruined the melons by the blight of a small black fly which the scientists found it impossible to recognize.

A particularly loathly annoyance whereby witches tormented their victims was through an uncouth spell to render them verminous. This filthy cantrip persists to-day. I have known the threat used and the dirty charm employed by sorcerers. In 1617 three Guernsey witches, Collette du Mont, her daughter Marie, and Isebel Becquet, were tried on multiplied charges. The household of James Gallienne, his wife and children had been cursed, and many other depositions of neighbours proved the accusation. Cattle died, mares miscarried, cows could give no milk, sheep sickened and fell, children and women were taken ill, men were lamed and palsied. There was no end to the mischief. Horrible black pimples broke out on the bodies of the afflicted persons; insects swarmed in their houses, and lice in such abundance that they had to be swept away with brooms. The witches were found guilty by the Royal Court of Guernsey of having practised the damnable art of sorcery and of having thereby caused the deaths of many persons, of having destroyed and injured much cattle, and of many other abominable crimes. They confessed, and were very justly strangled and burned at the stake.

At Bedford, about 1637, old Gammer Rose amongst other charges was accused of making "a man to be alwayes lowsie". The matter was proved beyond any question.

In 1645 a fearful witch, Elizabeth Fillet, of Witherenden, was put on her trial for various misdeeds. The wife of John Spink having made a slighting remark which was overheard by Mother Fillet, their child sickened and was suddenly covered with lice. In the same year Thomas Monticute refused old widow Thomazine Ratcliffe, of Shelley, some faggots. He became full of strange lice. A very respectable Norwich woman in 1843 made complaint before a magistrate that an old hag had bewitched her by sending her and her children a vast number of vermin. There dwelt as lately as 1874, in a lonely hut hard by the rugged promontory "La Roque du Guet", Caûbo Bay, Guernsey, a known witch of long continuance, who plagued the whole countryside by her spells. A woman scrupulously clean in her person and attire against whom the witch had a previous grudge chanced to make use of some not very complimentary expressions in speaking of the old hag, and instantaneously her clothes were covered with vermin of the most loathsome description.

A Guernsey lady, Miss E. Le Pelley, in 1896 related that two young fellows, still in their teens, one day happened to chaff an old woman, when suddenly she got furiously angry, and stooping down gathered a handful of dust which she flung in the air, at the same time gabbling a sentence very quickly. The boys went home, and found they were covered with vermin. One was so enraged that he took his gun, ran back to the witch's house, and levelling it at her cried: "Now rid me of the lice, or I will shoot you." The old wretch was really frightened. She took up some dust, scattered it on him, repeated some words, and the vermin disappeared. The other youth was worried for three days.

Mrs. Le Patourel, of St. Martin's, was told the following by the lady to whom it happened, her own mother-in-law, at the time of the incident Miss Mauger, of Saints. Miss Mauger and her sister, who came of a wealthy old family, went to school in England at a new fashionable academy, where they imbibed rather grand notions. On their return home, being very handsome girls and fond of gaiety, they used to go to all the country dances, and were much sought after as partners by the beaux of the Island. But as young ladies sometimes will they held their heads pretty high, and only cared to dance with the most select and most eligible gentlemen. One evening when they were present at a dance with a girl friend and all three happened to be particularly smartly dressed in new frocks, some man whom they did not know came up without any introduction and asked each of them in turn to dance with him. Each, however, refused rather coldly, letting it perhaps be seen a little too plainly that he was hardly the partner for them. He turned away muttering that they would soon repent their rudeness. A minute later one of the girls said to her sister, " Oh, Marie, whatever is that crawling on your lace ? " Red with confusion, the girl killed the insect, only to see swarms more moving over her white satin skirt. The other two girls to their horror found that they also were alive with vermin. In the utmost confusion all three hurriedly left the room, and hastened home. Do what they would they were plagued for three days, when the lice vanished as suddenly as they had appeared. Mrs. Le Patourel says that in telling the story her mother-in-law always concluded : " The shame of it I can never, never forget."

Mr. John de Garis, of Les Rouvets, comments : " I have heard of too many instances of this power of giving vermin being exercised to admit of doubt. The surprising part is the removal. I have not heard of a case for more than thirty years."

Dr. A. N. Symons, of Jersey, notes : " Several times I have heard that the Witches could cover a person with lice by magic. Miss R. V., who formerly lived with her people at Coin Varin, says that one of her brothers was troubled in this way by a witch who lived in the cottage, now ruined, beside Les Luanes Hill. He took a whip and threatened to thrash the witch, whereupon the trouble was removed."

Mr. John L. Amy, the author of *Jersey Folk Lore*, relates the following incident which was told him by his mother, who had it from the widow of the man who was bewitched. Jean L. was a farmer of some wealth and influence in his parish of St. Lawrence, and much respected throughout the whole district. It happened that he had to attend at Court on a certain Saturday to pass a contract which meant £400 to him, a business country folk were wont to complete with considerable preparation and ceremony. To visit the Royal Court on such an occasion was in fact a gala day, and necessitated donning Sunday clothes and every rustic formality. A few days before the great event there came to the farm begging for a pot of cider one Collas D., a shiftless and ill reputed vagabond, to whom incidentally the farmer had always refused alms. "Be off with you," cried the goodman with some vigour on seeing the ragged rascal at his gate. "Cider or Contract," was the reply. "Either you give me the cider or you do not go to the Court on Saturday." Jean L. laughed in the beggar's face. The important morning arrived, and spruced in his smartest toggery, swinging his black malacca cane with the silver head jauntily as he strode along, Maître Jean set out on his way to the Court. All was well until he had reached the top of Mont Cochon Hill, and he had actually forgotten the threat of Collas D. It felt good to be alive with a contract for some hundred pounds in one's pocket. And he was *alive* with a vengeance ! He began to twitch and itch. He halted, tore off his collar and set about scratching his neck and face. As he looked at his clothes he turned sick with horror and dismay. He saw that he was literally swarming with filthy vermin from head to foot. No help for it. He hurried back home by the short cut across the fields keeping in the shadow of the hedges lest anyone should see him. When he opened the door of his house the lice all vanished, not a trace was there to be seen. But it proved far too late to resume his journey.

In Cornwall some half a dozen years ago two men were ill-wished with vermin. The spell was broken by standing in a church porch on Sunday morning and muttering to themselves as the congregation was leaving : " We have lost our flocks, call them home."

The sterile witch-charm known as " Tying the points ", or in French *nouer l'aiguilette* :

                        to starve up generation,
To strike a barrenness in men and women,

so that the sexual functions in either sex were wholly incapacitated and a complete frigidity ensued was always regarded with especial abhorrence as an abomination mortally injurious to the most intimate human relations. Yet Delrio remarks that in his day it was one of the commonest as it was one of the vilest businesses of sorcery.

Bodin adds that there were no less than fifty methods of casting this accursed spell, which indeed is still employed by witches to-day, as a modern French writer, Roland Brévannes, attests.

The bond-slave of a murderer, the witch is also a murderer, a point that has already been touched upon, and one scarcely requiring any further enlargement. In Africa the ju-ju man will " hate " his enemy to death. The medicine doctor puts ju-ju on some person, and that person dies. He may fall down suddenly; he may waste inch by inch. Only because the wizard has looked at him, has pointed towards him, and willed him to die. That is all.

The German and Italian witches used to disinter human corpses, especially the bodies of criminals who had been hanged, to use them for the murderous slaughter of men. From such horrid material they confected charms of especial potency.

In the Navarrese witch-trials of 1610 Juan de Echelar confessed that a candle had been used made from the arm of an infant strangled before baptism. The ends of the fingers were lit, and burned with a clear flame.

The right hand of a gibbeted felon, severed at the wrist, was employed for the ghoulish charm known as the Hand of Glory; the Dead Man's Candle; or, the Corpse Candlestick. The instructions to fashion this magical taper are given at length in *Les Secrets du Petit Albert*. The ghastly relic of mortality was mummified by being placed in an earthen pot with coarse salt, dragon-wort, black pepper, nitre, and various spices. It was then bleached in the hottest noonday sun, or baked over a fire fed with bracken and vervain. Certain impious incantations accompanied the process. A candle having been moulded from the fat of a hanged murderer together with virgin wax and Lapland sesame the dead fingers were twisted so as to hold this horrible taper, which burned with a blue flame. Whilst this was alight all those in the house became entranced in a hypnotic sleep, and rendered incapable of word or movement. Housebreakers and assassins would purchase the Hand of Glory from witches at a high rate, and in the days when criminals were hanged in chains by the highway it was by no means impossible to procure the horrid ingredients for such a charm. There were, indeed, several recipes for it, and even to-day such practices are not unknown since it is authoritatively stated that in parts of Russia maidens have been killed in order to obtain the human fat for the manufacture of these necromantic candles. Madame de Baucé bought at a high price a Hand of Glory and a toad from the Parisian witch, La Voisin.

On the night of the 3rd January, 1831, a gang of Irish thieves broke into the house of Mr. Naper, of Loughcrew, Co. Meath. They had with them a dead man's hand with the fingers twisted round a candle. The servants, however, were alarmed and the robbers fled leaving the Hand of Glory behind them. It was suggested that it had not been exactly prepared, in which case the charm would certainly fail.

The witches, it must always be remembered, are adepts in the art of poisons, and no doubt the effect of their spells in many cases was not infrequently aided by a noxious draught. The devil, or Chief Officer of a coven, " delivers unto his *Proselite*, and so to the rest, the *Rules of his Art* instructing them in the manner of *hurting* and *helping*." Even John Webster whose *Displaying of Supposed Witchcraft* (1677), " utterly denied and disproved " " a *Corporeal League* made betwixt the Devil and the Witch ", is bound to acknowledge " secret poysoning, we grant to be too frequent and common, because those persons commonly accounted Witches are extreamly malicious and envious, and do secretly and by tradition learn strange poysons, philters and receipts whereby they do much hurt and mischief".

Among the minor, but very active, agents concerned in the scandals that came to a climax with the notorious poisoning of Sir Thomas Overbury in 1613 was " sweet father " Forman, as the Countess of Somerset used to call him, a professed sorcerer, astrologer, and necromancer, who vended curious philtres to the more wanton court ladies, and having obtained a licence from Cambridge University to practise medicine almost openly trafficked in poison. Mrs. Anne Turner, his daughter, who was hanged at Tyburn for her share in the murder, was at her trial frankly saluted by Sir Edward Coke as a bawd, a whore, a sorcerer, a witch, a felon, and a murderer.

Of the same kidney was Dr. John Lambe, " an absolute witch, a sorcerer, a juggling person given over to lewd, wicked, and diabolical courses, an invocator and adorer of impious and wicked spirits." Practising as a physician, he sold poisonous draughts of such graduated strength that a speedy or a slow death might be arranged according to his client's convenience. There can be little doubt that had it not been for the all-powerful protection of the Duke of Buckingham the Doctor would have been brought to Tyburn. He was so hated indeed that he dare not walk abroad in the streets of London, save in disguise. One afternoon in 1628 he ventured to visit the Fortune Theatre in Golden Lane to see a new play, but being recognized on his way home, a brutal mob attacked him and with hideous yells of " Kill the Duke's devil ! Kill the wizard ! Kill the poisoner ! " they beat him to death.

The Marquise de Brinvilliers and her paramour Sainte-Croix were continually consulting astrologers and warlocks with regard to the efficacy of their drugs and the right times to administer their arsenic and lunar caustic, for there is a propriety in these things. The gangs of witches directed by the Abbé Guibourg and Catherine La Voisin numbered many poisoners of the most approved and widest experience, physicians, chemists, apothecaries, who laid claim to being artists in their profession and were mighty proud of their feats.

In Rome the witch Hieronyma Spara dispensed a wonderful elixir, clear, tasteless, and limpid, which sent those who were obstructive—an aged parent, a cruel husband,—to their long last sleep. She was hanged on 5th July, 1659. Even more famous and more enterprising was her successor La Toffania, a Neapolitan witch, who seems to have distributed her drugs wellnigh all over Europe. By a horribly profane sleight she was wont to label her vials Manna of St. Nicolas of Bari ", so that they passed as the miraculous oil which exudes from the sacred tomb of St. Nicolas, and for reverence sake were unexamined. The *Aqua Toffania* appears to have been crystallized arsenic dissolved in large quantities of water with the addition (for some unexplained reason) of the herb cymbalaria. A few drops were generally poured into coffee, chocolate, or soup, and its effects, although deadly sure, were so slow as to be almost imperceptible.

When some victim is marked for death by the witch there is made of the doomed person an image or effigy of wax, clay, marl, lead, leather, wood, or almost any material, and this being pierced with black pins, nails, thorns, or even struck through with a knife or dagger is burned or slowly melted before a great fire. As the image is pricked so the victim suffers in that part of the body; as it is crumbled or dissolved, so he languishes; when it is melted away or pierced to the heart, he expires. Such are the theory and practice of this " sympathetic " or " homœopathic " magic, as it is sometimes known. The image thus fashioned for purposes of sorcery has many names : figurine, puppet, moppet, doll, baby (in the obsolete sense of " doll "), effigy, maumet (the same name as given to a familiar), simulacrum, or even picture, since a painted canvas, a portrait, may be effectually employed. If a lock of hair, a piece of clothing, the nail-parings, or some other substance intimately related to the victim can be secured and moulded in or attached to the poppet the charm acquires so much the more force and propulsion. Sometimes a heart, most frequently the heart of an animal, will be used instead of a figurine. Not very many years ago some new tenants who had taken a house in Somersetshire found hidden in the chimney a big black velvet heart with pins thrust through it. They heard that the house had belonged to a witch. Other substitutes are employed. In Somersetshire, again, a sorcerer will write his enemy's name on a piece of paper and fasten this with as many black pins as possible to an onion, which must be put up the chimney. As the onion shrivels and withers so will the victim languish. An onion treated thus was found in a cottage chimney about 1880. Not long ago in a churchyard at Bradford, Yorks, a lemon was discovered stuck full of pins. The Neapolitan witches pierce a lemon, an orange, a potato, with rusty nails or pins to cast sickness upon or to kill the person who has offended them. The Sicilian *strega* transfixes an egg, an orange, or a lemon to the same end.

Sometimes the malefic charm can be directed against the witch in return, as witness an instance that came to the notice of Lady Peirse, and which happened about ten years ago. In a certain south country village in England a local farmer whose cattle ailed most mysteriously and showed every sign of having been overlooked, whilst things in general went wrong with him in every direction, consulted the witch-doctor, and was told to repeat a certain rhyme last thing at night, to nail a sheep's heart to his front door, to lock and bolt the door, to fasten every window, to sit up alone and whatever might happen on no account so much as to lift the latch until morning. He did exactly as had been prescribed. The family all went to bed, and he commenced his lonely vigil by the kitchen fire. After about half an hour there came a loud knocking at the door, and a voice shouted: " Let me in ! Let me in for a moment." The farmer, although trembling and afraid, made no answer, and did not stir from his place. After a very short interval the knocking was repeated, and a deplorable voice in plaintive accents begged for the door to be opened, but the farmer, although it was all he could do not to rise and unlock the door, remained obdurate as he thought of his suffering beasts. Lastly there was heard a very feeble knocking and a dull moaning sound. The farmer, even more alarmed, stoutly kept his post until sunrise the next morning. When he opened the door a near neighbour lay stretched across his threshold, dead. The doctor pronounced it a case of sudden heart failure. Nobody could explain why the man should have come to the farmer's house, whilst the farmer alone of his family had heard the knocks. The cattle recovered in a most extraordinary way, and all other things too began to go smoothly and well.

Mrs. Carbonell knew a case which happened in Devonshire in 1925. D. had a valuable mare which died suddenly. The veterinary surgeon was frankly puzzled, and could only say that it must have been the heat. D., however, felt sure that the mare had been overlooked, and riding over to the near market town, he decided to consult the white witch. On entering the wise man's house, he was greeted with : " I know the business upon which you have come. Go home, cut out the mare's heart, and fill it as full as you can with pins, and the one who has forspoken you will die." The farmer on his return did as he had been bid, and within a very few weeks a certain neighbour, in the flower of his age, sickened and died, nor did the doctor give his illness any name save a decline.

The magic use of actual figurines, moulded from some plastic material in human form, reaches back to remotest antiquity to Egypt, to Assyria, Babylonia, and India. It has prevailed among all peoples, savage and civilized, and admits of almost infinite variants in preparation and performance.

From ancient Egypt the magic use of wax figures passed to Greece and thence to Rome. The Anglo-Saxon Penitential incorrectly ascribed to Ecgbert, Archbishop of York, punishes this kind of sorcery, and provides for heavier penalties if the victim dies. At the Colchester Summer Assizes of 1580 there were many indictments for witchcraft and conjuration of spirits. Amongst others Nicholas Johnson of Woodham Mortimer was charged with making the portrait in wax of Her Majesty Queen Elizabeth. Elizabeth Device, the Lancashire witch, made a clay picture of John Robinson and crumbled it away, and within a week the man died. In 1900 an Italian burned a wax figure of President McKinley, quilled with pins like a hedgehog, on the steps of the American Embassy in London. Image magic is common enough to-day here in England, and in all countries of the world.

In a sentence passed upon a knot of witches at Avignon in 1582, *A Summary of All the Crimes of Witches*, one article runs thus : " that the Father of Lies should have a care to delete and obliterate you from the Book of Life you did at his direction and command with your own hands write your names in the black book there prepared, the roll of the wicked condemned to eternal death ; and that he might bind you with stouter bonds to so great a perfidy and impiety, he branded each of you with his Mark as belonging to him."

The Devil's Mark to which allusion is here made, or the Witches' Mark, as it is sometimes called, was regarded as perhaps the chief point in the identification of a witch, it was the very sign and seal of Satan upon the actual flesh of his servant and any person who bore such a mark was considered to have been convicted and proven beyond all manner of doubt of being in league with and devoted to the service of the fiend. This mark was said to be entirely insensible to pain, and when pricked, however deeply, it did not bleed. So Mr. John Bell, minister at Gladsmuir, in his tract, *The Trial of Witchcraft; or Witchcraft Arraigned and Condemned*, published early in the eighteenth century, explains: "The witch mark is sometimes like a blew spot, or a little tate, or reid spots, like flea-biting; sometimes also the flesh is sunk in, and hollow, and this is put in secret places, as among the hair of the head, or eye-brows, within the lips, under the arm-pits, and in the most secret parts of the body." Robert Kirk, minister at Aberfoill, in his *Secret Commonwealth* (1691) writes: "A spot that I have seen, as a small mole, horny, and brown-coloured; throw which mark when a large pin was thrust (both in buttock, nose, and rooff of the mouth), till it bowed and became crooked, the witches both men and women, nather felt a pain nor did bleed, nor knew the precise time when this was doing to them, (their eyes only being covered)."

Thus in the case of the Guernsey witches who were convicted by the Royal Court in July, 1617, Isebell Le Moigne confessed one night that, when she was at the Sabbath, the Devil marked her on the thigh. "The mark thus made having been examined by women appointed for that purpose, they certified that they had thrust pins deep into it, and that Isebell felt no pain therefrom, nor did any blood follow when the pins were withdrawn."

Whilst the notorious French wizard, Louis Gaufridi, "Lucifer's lieutenant, and Prince of all the hosts of sorcerers from Constantinople to Paris," lay in prison at Marseilles two physicians and two surgeons were directed by the judges to search him for the devil's marks. In their report which is very technical and detailed they speak of having discovered three callous marks, which when probed gave no pain, and which from this and other signs they are bound to pronounce not to be natural.

Inasmuch then as the discovery of the devil-mark was regarded as one of the most convincing indications —if not indeed an infallible proof—that the accused was guilty, it is easy to see how the searching for, the recognition and the probing of, such marks actually grew to be a profession in which not a few ingenious persons came to be recognized as experts and practical authorities. In Scotland, especially, the " prickers ", as they were called, formed a regular gild. They received a good fee for every witch whom they discovered, and, as might be expected, they did not fail to reap a golden harvest. One of the most notorious was John Kincaid of Tranent, who was acknowledged a master in his craft, although he found a serious rival in John Bain, who also showed himself a whole-hearted enthusiast. About 1630 Mr. John Balfour, of Corhouse, was feared all over the country for his exploits, and proved so ardent a publicist that he eventually came under the notice of the Lords of the Privy Council, who finding that his knowledge " has only been conjectural " put an abrupt end to his activities. Yet some twenty years later one John Dick was energetically pursuing the pricker's profession. The regular trade of these " common prickers " came to be a serious nuisance, and confessedly opened the door to all sorts of roguery. There was a Mr. Paterson, " who had run over the kingdom for trial of witches. . . . This villain gained a great deal of money, having two servants ; at last he was discovered to be a woman disguised in man's clothes." In 1649 a Scotch pricker was called in at Newcastle-upon-Tyne, but the experiment hardly proved satisfactory. He charged twenty shillings for each subject, and eventually he turned out to be a mere cheat. In 1662 the Lords of His Majesty's Secret Council forbade any sort of pricking for witchcraft save it were done by special Order in Council, and within a very few months several prickers were sentenced to terms of imprisonment.

The fleeting upon the water, or as it is generally known, the " swimming " of a witch, the water-ordeal, was popularly considered to be so supremely efficacious a test that it was still in use, albeit wholly illegal, of course, among rustics as late as the nineteenth century. The witches tied with " their thumbs and great toes . . . acrosse " and steadied by ropes—(" a roape, tyed about their middles ")—were let down into the water, some running stream, or a pond. If she sank the suspect might be cleared ; if she swam her blackest guilt was evident. For water was a holy element, it had become instinct with life whilst the earth was yet barren and uninhabited ; and as the witch had rejected the sacramental water of Baptism, so the pure lymph would refuse to receive her into its bosom. The analogy is perfectly sound, and King James is quite correct when he writes : " It appeares that God hath apoynted (for a super-naturall signe of the monstrous impietie of the Witches) that the water shall refuse to receive them in her bosome, that have shaken off them the sacred Water of Baptisme, and wilfullie refused the benefite thereof." William Perkins of Cambridge, in his *Discourse of the Damned Art of Witchcraft*, posthumously published in 1608, endeavours to argue against this conclusion, by laying down that " The element out of the use of the Sacrament is no Sacrament, but returnes again to his common use", an opinion which much commends itself to a recent writer, who thus regards Perkins as having exploded the sacred character and symbolism of Holy Water. Perkins was no doubt a very grave and earnest author, but his theology (as here) is often extremely faulty, and it is because of this that the inference seems entirely to have escaped him. Holy Water is a sacramental, and possesses a particular efficacy of its own. It has, moreover, the virtue to drive away those evil spirits whose mysterious and baleful operations can do such harm to man. Baptismal water is especially sacrosanct, for it has been mixed with the holy chrism in solemn rite. It is not necessary to labour these points in detail, sufficient to remark how Perkins and his school have mistaken and are in error in this respect.

Actually the Ordeal by Swimming was the Judgement of God, and applied for many crimes. It goes back to very early days, about the sixth or seventh century, and it is obviously related to the belief that water (in particular running water "—A running stream they darena cross"—) will dissolve all enchantment and magic glamour. During the seventeenth century swimming was much favoured in England as a test for a witch, although it was seldom countenanced by authority. In 1612 two Bedfordshire witches were swum in a mill-dam by Master Enger, a "gentleman of worship", whom they had harmed, and they "floated like a plank". In the same year three Northamptonshire witches were swum, and could not sink. Examples might be multiplied. In some very few instances swimming was directed or at the least permitted by the local magistracy, but Bernard in his *Guide to Grand-Jury Men* insists upon the illegality of this test, and Hopkins who certainly favoured the process was soon forced to discontinue it.

There was living in 1931 at the Essex village of Good Easter, a man who in his youth had been in trouble with the local magistrates for attempting with his friends the trial by swimming of an old hag, who was generally believed to be a witch. She was, however, rescued from their hands before they had thrown her in the pool, and the charge brought against them resolved itself into that of attempting to do grievous bodily harm.

The *Morning Post* of 28th January, 1780, has an account of two old women of Beck's Hill (Bexhill), Sussex, suspected to be witches. Many of the leading inhabitants approached the parson, the lawyer, and the mayor, requesting that these beldames should be put to the test, " to try by swearing, swimming, or weighing them if the opinion of the people was well or ill founded." As it might have fared badly with the two women if this deputation had just been scouted, " the Clerk was dispatched for the Church Bible, which the two were weighed against, and which they out-weighed, *a sure proof they were not witches.*" This is an old experiment and one that was employed from time to time in country places, but it has never been officially recognized and can hardly be regarded as more than a tradition.

It has always been held that if the victim who is overlooked can draw blood from the witch the spell will be broken. Again and again we find in the records that in order to obtain relief the witch has been scratched or blooded. This occurs as early as 1279, when John de Warham was fined 12*d*. by the Leet Court at Lynn, Norfolk, for " blood draught on Fair Alice ", whom he had (it seems) wrongly suspected. Passing down more than six centuries we may note an experience related by Mr. Walter Britten, as happening to a friend of his who was making a stay at Sidmouth in the days when the modern bicycle was still something of a novelty. The visitor, an enthusiastic devotee of the wheel, had a new machine sent down from London, and locally became known as " the flying devil ". One evening, being waylaid in a lane near Sudbury by a number of rustics, he dismounted with no small misgiving. To his surprise the leader of the party ran a sharp pin into one of his legs chanting, " Prickee wi' a pin, and draw his blood, an' ee can't hurt ee ! " After which ceremony the whole company at once appeared quite satisfied and friendly. This, of course, was nothing else than the scratching of the witch, so continually spoken of in the old trials, and recognized by the demonologists as a powerful countercharm to malefic spells.

Writing from Plympton, on the 1st March, 1821, Lady Callcott (then Mrs. Graham) speaks of a rich baker in Plymouth, who some five years before had to pay five pounds compensation to a reputed witch. One of the baker's children being very sickly it was concluded the poor little creature had been overlooked, " and nothing but blood from the witch who had overlooked it could cure it. Accordingly, the lady of the Oven watched her opportunity ; and when the witch next came for a loaf, she and her maid flew on the old crone scratching her severely with long corking pins. The Mayor fined the baker, but it was considered extremely hard that a woman might not scratch a witch who had overlooked her child."

In August, 1927, an English lady who was walking in a wood near Travnik, in Bosnia, apparently aroused the suspicions of some peasant women, who crying out that she was a sorceress who would bewitch their children, attacked her, beating her and scratching her until the blood flowed. She escaped with difficulty, and found protection in the neighbouring village.

In 1928 a West Country smallholder was convicted of assaulting an old woman, whom he had scratched violently with a pin. The defence was that she had ill-wished him and his pig, so he had drawn blood on her to render her spells powerless to harm him for the future.

The black books or rolls of the witches carrying the names of the members of the coven were kept with great secrecy by the chief officer of the local society, or even by the Grand Master of a wider district. They would obviously have been guarded as something as precious as life itself, seeing that they contained the damning evidence of a full list of the witches of a province or county, and in addition thereto seems to have been added a number of magic formulæ, spells, charms, and probably, from time to time, a record of the doings of the various witches. The signing of such a book is continually referred to in the New England trials. So when Deliverance Hobbs had made a clean breast of her sorceries, " She now testifi'd that this *Bishop* [Bridget Bishop condemned and executed as a long-continued witch] tempted her to sign the *Book* again, and to deny what she had confess'd." The enemies of the notorious Matthew Hopkins made great capital out of the story that by some sleight of sorcery he had got hold of one of these Devil's memorandum-books, whence he copied a list of witches, and this enabled him to be so infallible in his scent.

An old Yarmouth witch in 1645 described how one night she heard a knock at her door, and peeping from her window she saw in the moonlight a tall, black man, whom she admitted. After some parley he promised to help her under certain conditions, and taking a little penknife he scratched her hand so that the blood flowed, with which she wrote her name in his book, and he guided her fingers.

Anne Bodenham, sometime servant to the notorious warlock, Dr. John Lambe, was executed at Salisbury when 80 years old. She had many books of spells, and especially a red one " written half over with blood, being the names of witches that had listed themselves under the Devil's command ". This, however, could not be recovered as it had been sent for safe keeping to a wizard named Withers, who lived near Romsey, Hants, and who absconded.

There is a somewhat vague story, no dates being given, that a Devil's book was carried off by Mr. Williamson of Cardrona (Peebles), who filched it from the witches whilst they were dancing on Minchmoor. But the whole coven at once gave chase, and he was glad to abandon it and escape alive.

Sometimes the catalogue of witches was inscribed on a separate parchment, and the book only used to write down charms and spells. Such a volume was the Red Book of Appin known to have actually been in existence a hundred years ago. Tradition said that it was stolen from the Devil by a trick. It was in manuscript, and contained a large number of magic runes and incantations for the cure of cattle diseases, the increase of flocks, the fertility of fields. This document, which must be of immense importance and interest, when last heard of was (I believe) in the possession of the now extinct Stewarts of Invernahayle. This strange volume, so the story ran, conferred dark powers on the owner, who knew what inquiry would be made even before the question was poised ; and the tome was so confected with occult arts that he who read it must wear a circlet of iron around his brow as he turned those mystic pages.

It is a strange and not very edifying chance which has popularly attached the names of great Popes and Saints to books of spells and grimoires, and some authors such as Father Delrio, Pierre Le Loyer, and Gabriel Naudé, the learned librarian of Cardinal Richelieu and Cardinal Mazarin, have been at the pains to show how absurd and indeed scandalous such attributions are. There is no need to labour the point, for of course nobody imagines that Honorius III composed an infernal grimoire or that St. Albert the Great is the author of a manual giving directions how to prepare cabbalistic talismans and a ring conferring invisibility, any more than we believe (as was once seriously asserted) that Abel wrote a treatise on judicial astrology, which he enclosed in a rock where after the Deluge it was discovered and published by the patriarch Noah.

The history with the ancillary bibliography of grimoires and books of spells is immense and immensely complicated, nor even if it were desirable to treat so dangerous a subject would it be possible to discuss it save at very considerable length. In order to illustrate the witches' library I will do no more then than mention a very few works which are so notorious that no purpose could be served by ignoring them, whilst no harm can come from so slight and guarded a notice.

Among the oldest and most terrible of the grimoires is the *Sepher Toldos Jeschu*, a Syro-chaldaic work, whose pages are happily sealed save to the very few. A book of conjurations, *Ars Notaria*, was once printed under the name of St. Jerome. Owing to a confusion between St. Cyprian, Bishop of Carthage, and St. Cyprian of Antioch the coverted sorcerer, who was martyred fifty years later, a number of mediæval spells have been ascribed to the former. Thus in Denmark and Scandinavia among the witches to-day almost any grimoire is dubbed the *Book of Cyprianus*. St. Ubald, Bishop of Gubbio in the twelfth century, who was especially famous for his powers in casting out evil spirits, is named on the title-page of a theurgical treatise which cannot be earlier than four centuries after his death. In France in the days of the Valois they were selling all sorts of alchemical and magical opuscules as being from the pen of St. Thomas Aquinas, upon whose venerable preceptor, St. Albert the Great, have been fathered perhaps the most famous, or most infamous, of all printed grimoires, *Les admirables Secrets du Grand Albert*, and the collection known by the running title *Le Petit Albert*, which two are the most extensively employed, and in some ways the most mischievous, grimoires to-day. It must be borne in mind that the numerous editions and reprints, both of

Le Grand Albert and *Le Petit Albert*, vary very widely, so much so, in fact, that a modern copy may be an entirely different book from an eighteenth century duodecimo carrying either name, whilst a third collection in its turn will present something quite new. Thus the 1668 sextodecimo, printed at Lyons, has charts of necromantic figures, talismans and pentacles, which are to be found in no other issue. (There is a facsimile, made about thirty years ago.) Add to this that for the most part the two books were clandestinely given to the Press, often without printer's name, the place incorrectly stated, a fudge imprint in fine, and it will be seen how perplexed the whole story is. Some editions are comparatively harmless; silly maybe, and even superstitious; others have deadly and dangerous pages.

The *Grand Albert* (as we know it) was possibly first printed about the middle of the sixteenth century, but the eighteenth century editions (of the last rarity) are considered the most complete. The *Petit Albert* was joined with the *Grand Albert* in one volume and edited (1885) by a well-known French occultist, Marius Decrespe. This is said to be the issue most prized by adepts to-day. Decrespe emphatically discredits the opinions of those who suggest that the dual work originated in any sense with St. Albert the Great, or was compiled by a student of the fifteenth century from an unedited manuscript of the learned Dominican doctor. It is almost certain that the two works as we now have them were an amalgamation of the discoveries of several individuals, and that they appeared at Lyons not earlier than the sixteenth century. Stanislas de Guaita drew attention to the fact that in spite of the many reprints both the *Grand* and the *Petit Albert* are very uncommon books.

In the Channel Islands the *Grand Albert* is known as the " Witches' Bible ", and local dialect terms it *Le Grand Mêlé*. The *Petit Albert* is *Le Petit Mêlé*, the word *Mêlé* signifying nothing more than " book ". Together they are often referred to as *Albins*, and only the sorcerer dare keep such " bad books ". There have been many cases of the two volumes appearing in various libraries which were being catalogued after the owner's decease, and such an accident is always regarded as throwing a strange light upon the character and pursuits of the defunct. The old wives say that once a man has owned the *Grand Albert* he cannot rid himself of it, do what he will. The book invariably returns to its place on the shelf, even if it be cast into a fire, thrown away at sea, torn to pieces and scattered to the winds. The only thing to do is to inter it in a grave, and read the burial service over the place, or else to get a priest to drench the accursed thing with holy water and burn it with litany and prayer.

In Jamaica when Monteul Edmond was arrested for the murder of Rupert Mapp, a boy of 12 years old, for purposes of obeah it was found that the body had been strangely mutilated and a search of the prisoner's person discovered a number of magical formulæ " copied from a work entitled *Petit Albert* the pretended author of which is claimed to be a monkish occultist of the Middle Ages ".

The Daily Gleaner, Kingston, Jamaica, on 30th January, 1934, among the police news reported that at the Sandy Bay Court, Leonard Weakley, of Cold Spring, was sentenced to six months' imprisonment for practising the black art. In his house were found the following books : *The Sixth and Seventh Books of Moses; Albertus Magnus, or the White and Black Arts for Men and Beasts; The Great Book of Black Magic; The Book of Magical Art; Hindoo Magic and Indian Occultism.*

It was stated during the John H. Blymyer trial (1928) at York, York County, Pennsylvania, that the principal "witchcraft guises" employed by the sorcerers are : The Sixth and Seventh Books of the Magical Spirit ; The Art of Moses, popularly known as The Black Art Bible ; Heaven's Letter (Himmelsbrief) ; and The Long-lost Friend, which contains the necromantic rituals and the creed of pow-wowism. *The Art of Moses* is a translation, or adaptation of the *Magia divino-mosaica . . . cum nigromantia* of the sixteenth century. All these grimoires are very rare and the possession of one or two confers a certain distinction upon the witch.

The *Enchiridion* of Pope Leo III, fabled to have been presented by that great Pontiff to the Emperor Charlemagne in the year 800 is, of course, purely apocryphal. There is an early edition of 1584, and the Mainz edition of 1633 has woodcuts in black and red, but the 16mo edition "*chez le Père Angelo de Rimini*" (Paris, 1847), presents ten coloured plates of pentacles, magic circles, seals engraved with words of power, and other curious matter, such as counter-spells to divert malefic enchantments. Upon the title-page is a triangle in a double circle with Hebrew characters, *Tsabaoth Alchim*, etc., inscribed in the midst.

The grimoires need not for their contents detain us. *The Grimoire of Pope Honorius* is said to be found in manuscript at least as early as the thirteenth century.

It was printed at Rome in 1629, and has several times been reissued. The edition of 1670 has many magical and cabbalistic figures, for this volume of witchcraft is chiefly concerned with the evocation of demons.

The *Grand Grimoire* and the *Grimorium Verum* are both to a large extent derived from the famous *Clavicula Salomonis, The Key of Solomon the King*, sometimes known as the *Book of the Pentacles*. The legend of a manual of black magic written by Solomon and confided to his son Rehoboam (Roboam) is very ancient. Mr. S. L. M. Mathers, who translated *The Key of Solomon the King* in 1889, says : " I see no reason to doubt the tradition which assigns the authorship of the *Key* to King Solomon." This view, however, cannot be accepted without very considerable qualification, for it is abundantly evident that the *Key*, in any form as we now have it, must have been altered and amplified (and possibly in some particulars retrenched) by those through whose hands it passed. It is safer to allow that the *Key* is substantially based upon immemorial tradition, much of which may go back to the time of Solomon, but that it has suffered various modifications in the course of the centuries without indeed affecting its essential character and design.

It is true that *The Key of Solomon the King* has been claimed to be a work of white magic, but since (to mention no further examples) it teaches how to describe a pentacle causing ruin, utter destruction, and death, whilst another pentacle is productive of earthquakes and great storms, this pretence—for it is plainly nothing more—cannot be maintained. For obvious reasons the malefic nature of a grimoire would often have been dissembled. Moreover the manuscript grimoires are in general far more detailed and far more terrible than the printed volumes, bad enough in all conscience though the latter may be. The sorcerer dare not confide the darker secrets of his evil craft, the more potent and perilous spells to what is after all—however limited the number of copies—a certain method of publication. The compositors might be heavily bribed, nay, they might even themselves be members of the Satanic fraternity, but there would always remain the chance that by some accident a copy of a printed book might fall into hostile hands and the mine be sprung. In past centuries this must have been an even more imminent risk than to-day. Very often in the printed manuals a slight difference has been deliberately made in an exorcism, some little variant occurs in a ceremonial, lest the horrid science should be too plainly betrayed to the uninitiated and the intruder. The adept who is using the book will appreciate this policy of reticence and heed the signs of caution; from his own training and the oral lessons he has received he can correct such divergences, and that is the reason why these mystic manuals are so often scored with manuscript emendations and so copiously annotated in their broad margins.

It has been said that wellnigh every witch of long continuance or standing possessed *The Key of Solomon the King*, and generally in a manuscript written out by himself. The advantage of this is obvious, for he could add any number of incantations and charms which he had been taught by word of mouth. In the time of Louis XIV, Duprat, a Parisian schoolmaster who was not unconnected with the Guibourg-La Voisin gang, enjoyed a very pretty living by transcribing and writing out grimoires. In the eighteenth century the Marquis de Paulmy, a deep student of occultism, made a large collection of manuscript grimoires, which are now preserved in the Bibliothèque de l'Arsenal at Paris. One of the most complete of these is entitled *The Great Secret, or the Key of Solomon the King and the Ancient Grimoire*, being, as indeed is indicated by the very name, a work combining the *Clavicula* with the *Grimoire of Pope Honorius*. Although actually it does not present a large number of figures and charts of circles it does describe many ceremonies and charms not to be found elsewhere. Dating from the early part of the eighteenth century, it is written in a very legible and elegant hand, and was evidently penned with the greatest care throughout. A note initialed by the Marquis de Paulmy says that no Hebrew manuscript of *The Key of Solomon* has ever been traced. Moreover Greek manuscripts are of the last rarity. Indeed only one was certainly known, and that reposed in the library of Charles Albert of Bavaria. Latin versions were not altogether infrequent. The manuscript actually is in French. It commences with a Preface, which does not occur in any other copy, wherein Solomon confides his *Key* to his son Rehoboam, in accordance with the old tradition. The book is supposed to have been found in Solomon's tomb, and the ivory coffer in which it was contained hence came into the possession of a Babylonian mage, who gave it to the world's philosophers. Leaving all legends aside, there is at least one salutary cautel added to the foreword. The author or transcriber, whoever he may be, is very insistent in his word of warning : " I conjure and I beseech any man into whose hands this manuscript may fall, I implore him by all that is holy, by his desire for good success in all his business and doings, that he shall never turn this book to any common use, that he shall neither publish it abroad, nor generally disclose the secrets hereof, nor translate it into the vulgar tongue, but to show it only to and to suffer it only to be seen by men who have understanding and who are well-tried and knowing in these rare secrets."

The earlier chapters of the *Key* describe in detail those preliminary ceremonies and rituals which are necessary for the successful invocation of spirits, a thing not to be embarked upon lightly or without due preparation and care. The *Key* will have it that the spirits who shall appear in these circumstances are benign influences, and but rarely evil, and these latter should be approached most circumspectly. The Christian Faith admits no such distinctions. However kindly and plausible they may seem to be we know that all such conjured spirits are demons of the pit.

As Mr. A. E. Waite has justly observed : " Much that passed current in the west as White (i.e. permissible) Magic was only a disguised goeticism, and many of the resplendent angels invoked with divine rites reveal their cloven hoofs. It is not too much to say that a large majority of past psychological experiments were conducted to establish communication with demons, and that for unlawful purposes. The popular conceptions concerning the diabolical spheres, which have all been accredited by magic, may have been gross exaggerations of fact concerning rudimentary and perverse intelligences, but the wilful viciousness of the communicants is substantially untouched thereby."

Full details of the vestments which must be donned by the charmer are supplied, and he should even wear a particular kind of buskin or shoe ; he must furnish himself with such accessories as a keen knife or whinger ; a long needle or cobbler's awl ; a ring ; a wand ; fire ; holy water ; lights ; certain sweet perfumes ; virgin parchment and a quill never yet used ; ink, and a phial of blood wherewith to write ; which things are absolutely indispensable for the operation since to summon a familiar spirit is no light and simple business as idle and silly meddling folk might suppose.

The manuscript gives an elaborate plan of the magic circle which is to be found in every manual of sorcery and in which unless he will risk the most imminent peril, even death itself, the experimenter must take his stand. This detail is emphasized in all grimoires, and the manuscript admonishes : "Note well that the mage who invokes the spirits must take his place within the circle, nor let him stir thence." The circle which was to measure nine feet in diameter, must be traced with the sharp point of the consecrated knife, and (the rubrics direct) : "having drawn this circle describe four Pentacles whereabouts are to be written the Holy Names of God, and without this circle describe yet another circle which shall be bounded by a square. Grave all these with thy knife's point."

Actually both Greek and Hebrew characters are traced about the circle and pentacles. Alpha, Omega, can be clearly distinguished ; as well as the mystic word *Agla*, which was used by the rabbis as signifying *Aieth Gadol Leolam Adonai*, Adonai (God Almighty) endureth throughout all ages. There are also written several of the seventy and two Names of God.

However, in different editions and manuscripts of *The Key of Solomon* the circle is varied, and in one ceremony the hierophant is required to have an attendance of four acolytes. Five circles are then traced, the first being greater than the rest, in which the master takes his position. The disciples stand appropriately in the smaller circles. All must be clothed in ephods of stainless white linen, and the master whilst he draws the circles recites the following psalms : II, (Why do the heathen rage,) ; LIV, (Save, me, O God, by Thy Name) ; CXII, (Praise ye the Lord) ; LXVII, (God be merciful unto us) ; XLVII, (O clap your hands, all ye people) ; and LXVIII, (Let God arise . . .). A number of other circles and pentacles having been described, the Four Great Names of God must be written around and about, to wit in the small circles, Adonai, El, Agla, and Jah, and in the larger circle Eloha, Ehie, Elijon, and the mystic Tetragrammaton, that is the Divine Name, the Name of Yahweh, which no man may pronounce (saith Rabbi Abba Shaul) and live, the separated, the hidden and mysterious Name, inscribed here in such manner as may reverently and fearfully be spoken.

Another manuscript of the *Key of Solomon*, now in the Bibliothèque de l'Arsenal, *The True and Only Key of King Solomon*, said to be translated from the Hebrew in the eighteenth century, instructs the experimenter to draw his circle in quite a different fashion. Similar names, however, are to be written, the central monogram being KIS, which stands for *Kadosh Ieve Sabaoth*, Holy Lord of Hosts.

Although as yet unpublished, there is preserved in a private English collection a manuscript translation of the *Clavicula Salomonis* by Frederick Hockley, an astrologer and occultist who died about the middle of the last century. It is entitled " Solomon's Key, by Frederick Hockley, 1828 ". Pasted inside the cover is a paper carrying the following : " Magia de Profundis, seu Clavicula Salomonis Regis, the Key of Solomon the King, or a Complete System of Profound Magical Science with a great number of coloured drawings of the Characters of the Spirits Seals, Pentacles, etc., elegant in brown calf gilt leaves." At the beginning we have : " Key of Solomon in Four books. These books were found in the Chaldee and Hebrew tongue by a Jewish Rabbi at Jerusalem & by him translated into Greek & from thence into Latin and transcribed by Fred^k Hockley the first day of Marche 1828."

The Bibliothèque de l'Arsenal has manuscripts of a yet more profoundly dangerous kind than even the more extreme examples of the group which conveniently goes under the name of *The Key of Solomon*. Thus *The True and Only Key*, to which reference has already been made, provides a curious rose-form pentacle expressly to invoke the demons of the pit. The Great Conjuration contained in another manuscript is full of horrible impiety, and may justly be styled the Dark Secret of Secrets. *The Evocation of the Seven Planetary Spirits* prescribes that certain substances, chiefly storax and benjamin are to be burned in a new censer, and I remember J. K. Huysmans saying how a devil-worshipper had once told him that the fume of these two was " agreeable to Satan our master ".

The Conjuration of Uriel and the Seraphim has the most elaborate and reticulated plans and pentacles, and among other spirits honour is paid to Alithael, Cassiel,

Sachiel, and Samael. The angel St. Uriel " Regent of the Sun "

The sharpest sighted Spirit of all in Heav'n, as Milton terms him, is mentioned in the Fourth Book of Esdras, and other ancient writings, but the names Cassiel and others too plain betray the cloven hoof.

In Francis Barrett's *The Magus; or, Celestial Intelligencer*, 1801, is given a specimen of the Book of Spirits, being the Conjuration of Saturday in ceremonial magic; the Ruler, Cassiel. Here then we are in the realms of demonism undisguised.

Samael is Satan, the arch-fiend, as Collin de Plancy explicitly states, whilst Stanislas de Guaita says that Samael is opposed to and fought with the Archangel, Saint Michael.

Another manuscript, entitled *Zekerboni*, was written by Pietro Mora, who describes himself as an " occult philosopher ". During the Great Plague which so fearfully ravaged Milan in 1630 there was dwelling in an obscure quarter Pietro Mora, a mysterious and formidable figure, who had long been popularly accused as a vendor of poisons and a witch. A surprise visit searched his house, but the *sbirri* could trace nothing extraordinary or incriminating until almost by chance there was forced a secret panel masquing the entrance to cellars of prodigious extent, and in these vaults were discovered not only the horrid paraphernalia of sorcery, magic robes and wands, lamps, swords, tripods, thuribles, braziers, curiously graven shew-stones and crystals, together with a whole library of grimoires and Ephesian runes, but also a vast number of sealed jars and carefully labelled phials containing liquids and chemical preparations, which upon being analysed by the physicians were pronounced to be virus and poisons of the most deadly kind. Mora confessed that he was the leader of a coven of sorcerers, who had leagued themselves to spread the scourge and destroy the entire city. This they did by smearing the handles of doors and gates with a certain lethal ointment. They poisoned the springs of water, the fountains in the squares, and even the benitiers in the church porches. They distributed under the guise of charity infected clothing and foul linen from the beds of those who had died of the disease among the hospitals and the crowded warrens of the poor so that the pestilence was fearfully increased. The whole knot were apprehended and being convicted upon most plain and detailed evidence, they paid the extreme penalty of the law. The very house of Mora, as a criminal of especial atrocity, was razed to the ground, and a column erected on the spot with an inscription to commemorate his guilt.

There can be little question that Pietro Mora of Milan was the author or transcriber of *Zekerboni*, although it does not necessarily follow that the manuscript which has been preserved is his original. It may be a copy, and indeed it seems to be in a later hand. A circumstance which makes the identification more probable is that *Zekerboni* introduces into many of the spells certain terms and expressions borrowed from alchemy, and we know that Mora long sought the elixir and the philosopher's stone.

Zekerboni has a drawing of the " Great Pentacle " where four circles enclose a mesh of cryptic designs, crossing and recrossing, and scattered with Hebrew and Greek letters punctuated by curious sigils and points. The ceremony commences thus : " After the Master is come with his disciples to the appointed place of evocation he shall strike fire, and he shall exorcize the new fire wherewith he shall light the magic candle. This must be set in the lanthorn which must be held by one of the disciples so that the Master may most conveniently read the conjurations. Another disciple shall hold him ready with paper, a pen and the ink ; a third disciple shall carry the consecrated sword with naked blade. The Master shall light the charcoal for the censing and the fumigations. When he hath taken his stand within the circle, holding a lighted taper in his left hand, he shall forthwith begin the conjuration—." The formula which, it is recommended, shall be very legibly inscribed upon a fair parchment without blot or erasure differs in the various manuals. Each have certain phrases in common. The Holy Name of God is called upon, and most spells require the demon to manifest himself " in a pleasing form, without any horror of shape or size, without any loud or thunderous noise or alarum, without seeking to harm him who summons thee, and without hurting any who are of his company ".

When the spirit appears the magician must impose his commands upon him, and then give him licence to depart. The dismissal of the spirit is a very essential detail in the ceremony, for unless the demon is sent away it 'is possible that he may linger and great mischief may ensue. One form of concluding the rite is : " Depart then, gracious and kindly spirit, return in peace unto thy dwelling-place and unto thine own habitation, but yet do thou hold thyself ready to attend and appear before me whensoever I call upon thee and summon thee in the name of the Great Alpha, the Lord. Amen. Amen. Amen." It will be noticed how cunningly fair-spoken and even pious phrases are employed to masque the impiety of this horrid business.

Occasionally a manuscript grimoire will appear in the sale rooms. In April, 1934, part of the collection of M. Lionel Hauser was put up to auction at Sotheby's. There were many items of exceptional interest. A Treatise of Ceremonial Magic, written on vellum in cypher in French, *circa* 1750, which had belonged to and been used by the Comte de St. Germain, fetched £42 10s., whilst a nineteenth century manuscript collection of spells, conjurations, and exorcisms, realized £10.

In their great Catalogue of Medicine, Alchemy, Astrology, published in 1929 (No. 520), Messrs. Maggs, the well-known London booksellers, included " A Manuscript Book of Black Magic written in Shakespeare's England ", which was further very accurately described as " An Elizabethan Devil-worshipper's Prayer-Book ". The date assigned is *circa* 1600, but there seems to be no clue to the identity of the compiler of the manuscript, which is written on twenty-three leaves of vellum and illustrated with thirteen crudely drawn but very powerful drawings, some of which are coloured, of the demon king Vercan, who is pictured under various forms. There are also six other drawings of demons. All of these have their several invocations on the opposite page, inscribed in Latin. The spirits to be summoned or exorcised are : Vercan, Maymon, Suth, Samax, Sarabotres, Mediac or Modiac, and Arcan. King Vercan, who is regarded as the most powerful of the demons, is called upon in thirteen prayers. He is shown as a kind of semi-human monster with a fearfully grotesque human face, horned, having a hairy body, and the feet of a bird of prey. Twice he appears with three heads, and once he is riding a bear. It should be remarked that the invocator is always surrounded by a magic circle, for indeed as a later enchanter has it, "the circles are certain fortresses," and no manifestation has power to break through these boundaries, although often the spirits will endeavour to tempt or force the operator out of the circle.

The other demons of the grimoire are: King Maymon, who appears as a black familiar with two bird-heads, and two human heads at his knees. He rides upon a dragon, and is linked with the planet Saturn. King Suth is brown. Wearing a diadem and flourishing a great sword, he bestrides a stag, and is companioned with Jupiter. King Samax is antlered, and rides a kind of panther. He is linked with Mars. King Sarabotres is green. He rides a roe, and wields a sceptre. His planet is Venus. King Mediac (or Modiac) has huge horns. Clad in red mail, he rides a bear, and is linked with Mercury. King Arcan is a black demon with flaming eyes and grinning fangs. He is hunting with bow and arrows on the back of a roebuck. His planet is the Moon.

It very infrequently happens that there is any mention of a grimoire in a contemporary trial. John Walsh, of Netherbury, Dorset, possessed a book left him by his late master, which had great circles in it, wherein he would set two wax candles and a cross of virgin wax, to raise the familiar spirit of whom he would then ask for anything stolen. When his book

THE DEMON KING MAYMON

was taken from him he could no longer summon a familiar. Rebecca West, an Essex witch, met with some other witches by appointment at the house of Elizabeth Clarke, where they all spent some time praying to their familiars, and afterwards some read in a book belonging to Elizabeth, whereupon the said familiars did appear.

A Magic book, which formerly belonged to Dr. John Caius, the famous Cambridge scholar, is preserved in the British Museum.

Dr. John Harries (1785–1839), a celebrated Welsh physician and seer who dwelt at Cŵrt-y-Cadno, a hamlet in remotest Carmarthenshire, but who was resorted to by the whole countryside, possessed a great Book of Magic which none but the wizard himself might read with impunity. The Book, indeed, was always kept locked, because (as the thaumaturge was wont to say) if any ignorant person who knew not the mystic mantra were to turn its pages he might let loose unreined influences ready to destroy him. Many wonderful stories are told of Harries, and there seems no reason to doubt that he was an occultist of extraordinary power. He openly avowed that his knowledge of future and distant things was imparted to him by familiar spirits, and his son Henry, who succeeded him, inherited his father's mysterious gifts. Henry died in 1849. He specialized in astrology, having in his youth been apprenticed to the well-known astrologer Raphael of London. Some said that the notorious Book was actually not a book at all, but a number of papers kept in an iron-bound box, which the doctor regarded as of the utmost value. So perhaps it was a manuscript grimoire. One story went that many years after the death of the Welsh wizard and his sons, the book and a magic crystal were bought from his descendants by a London barrister on a walking tour, who having heard of the fame of Harries visited the village. The family parted with the Book and the crystal at a price, but nobody in the house dare touch them or would lend a hand in their removal.

There is to-day (1933) a wise man dwelling near Llangwrig, Montgomeryshire, who is famous throughout all Wales. From near and far people come for his help. He breaks the spells of those bad folk " who have power ", that is to say witches. In a rosewood box he keeps two books, an almanac and another, whereby he can divine and cast a horoscope or map out the planets for his clients.

Upon the black roll of magicians stands no more notorious name than that of Cornelius Agrippa, and there seems little doubt that this terrible accusation is in great part due to his youthful treatise, the *Three Books of Occult Philosophy*. Even Professor Henry Morley when writing his *Life of Henry Cornelius Agrippa von Nettesheim, Doctor and Knight*, added on the title-page " Commonly known as a Magician ". Composed in 1510, not even the First Book was printed until one and twenty years later, and when after about another twelvemonth it was announced that the whole work was in the press at Cologne, Conrad Cöllin, a learned Dominican of Ulm, very justly caused the book to be thoroughly examined by the theologians before it was given to the public. So far from being an obscurantist Cöllin was the most liberal of scholars, and there was no persecution or oppression. Satisfied that it contained no heresies, he gave his formal consent to the issue of the work. "Suffer it to be printed, if they wish," he says in an extant letter. Since the *Occult Philosophy* has been analysed in some detail by Morley it will suffice to say here that the work is a commixture of Neoplatonism and the Cabbala. The last book has a long chapter on demons, and there is a good deal of angelology with some curious matters that skate on very thin ice. Indeed these *Three Books of Occult Philosophy*, or rather of Magic, for Agrippa himself confessed that his title was little more than a subterfuge, " alone constitute him a conjurer "—the phrase is Morley's.

It is all the more unfortunate that after Agrippa's death there should have appeared an abominably superstitious and profane Fourth Book of the *Occult Philosophy*, whilst in the same volume was printed a fitting companion, the *Elements of Magic* by Peter of Abano, that " vilest of vile books ", to which reference has already been made. It is significant that those responsible for seeing these grimoires through the press did not dare to give the place or the printer's name on the title-page.

In spite of his virtuous and emphatic protestations it is impossible to regard Francis Barrett's *The Magus; or, Celestial Intelligencer* as anything other than a particularly elaborate and complete grimoire. Published in 1801 by a well-known firm, James Lackington, Allen and Co., at the " Temple of the Muses ", Finsbury Square, *The Magus*, a fine quarto, is illustrated with a number of detailed designs of magic circles and pentacles, and also with several striking coloured plates, the *Powers of Evil*, being heads of

Demons, Astaroth, Abaddon, Mammon, and *Vessels of Wrath*, Theutus, Asmodeus, and the Incubus. Barrett not only sketched the heads himself with great care, but he supplies a very ample account of the familiar shapes and forms in which the spirits manifest themselves, " likewise the whole perfection of magical ceremonies is here described syllable by syllable." " The Construction and Composition of all Sorts of Magic Seals, Images, Rings, Glasses, etc.," may be found exhibited in these pages. The author, who lived at 99 Norton Street, Marylebone, in an advertisement invites those desiring to delve further into these curious matters to join his school " which will consist of no greater number than Twelve Students ", an extremely significant circumstance. The manuscript of *The Magus*, which is preserved in a private collection, enlarges upon certain particulars not altogether desirable to print, and Barrett stands forth as a magician self-confessed.

The rough woodcuts which embellish such manuals of sorcery as *Le Dragon rouge*, *La Poule Noire*, and *Le Dragon Noir* have little importance. None the less both *Le Dragon rouge* and *La Poule Noire*, which first appeared in print about 1800, have been reissued again and again, and are yet extensively consulted and employed. They are grimoires of the worst type, and even furnish necromantic evocations.

During the Helsingfors Satanist scandals of 1931, when it was discovered that a number of graves had been desecrated and bodies mutilated, upon the arrest of the cemetery caretaker, Sarrenheimo, and the search of his house it was found that he possessed a library of books dealing with the practice of the black art, and one manual in particular (said to have been printed in England) advised the use of human remains in confecting certain foul charms.

There are in use by witches to-day volumes simply entitled *Magick*, which give the full ritual for the celebration of Black Masses, with diabolic litanies, and other infernal ceremonies including the blood sacrifices on the altar. A Gnostic Mass is described, and one rubric runs, "the blood sacrifice is the critical point of the World Ceremony of the Proclamation of Horus, the Crowned and Conquering Child, as Lord of the Aeon." The Gnostics in the second century had books "full of wickedness", and stripped of its pseudo-mystical verbiage the plain meaning of this rubric is that divine honour must be paid to the devil, Satan-Pantheus, with whom (Stanislas de Guaita says) St. Michael fought victoriously for he it is whom they salute as the Child, the Cosmic serpent who tempted Eve and by whom came death and sin.

One of these grimoires has this warning: "The student, if he attains any success in the following practices, will find himself confronted by things too glorious or too dreadful to be described. It is essential that he remain the master of all that he beholds, hears, or conceives; otherwise he will be the slave of illusion and the prey of madness."

Éliphas Lévi, whose two great works *Dogme de la Haute Magie* (1855) and *Rituel de la Haute Magie* (1856) were together translated in 1923 as *Transcendental Magic* by Mr. Arthur Edward Waite, lays down five *Conditions of Success in Infernal Evocations*: (1) Invincible obstinacy; (2) a conscience at once hardened to crime and not subject to remorse and fear ; (3) ignorance, affected or natural ; (4) blind faith in all that is incredible ; (5) a completely false idea of God. If these are understood in the right way they may be regarded as sufficiently summing up the essential characteristics of black magic and all goetic experiments. By *a completely false idea of God* I understand the express renunciation of God, the paying of divine honour to Satan with whom a contract (tacit or explicit) is made and whose will is done by the witch.

It must ever be borne in mind that the practice and profession of black magic are not lightly to be undertaken ; the dark mysteries are no jest, no pastime of an idle hour as many fools and empty inquirers seem to suppose. There are no dilettanti in witchcraft.

There are the mountebanks, of course, who give fatuous talks on black magic in Mayfair drawing-rooms ; there are the bright young things who try to raise the devil in a circle and do not succeed ; there is the fifth-rate novelist who peppers his trashy thrillers with occult episodes borrowed *en bloc* from some standard work. There is and there always will be plenty of humbug, and very paying humbug too, along these lines.

Before the secrets of the grimoire can be unfolded the price must be given, the terrible barter must be exchanged.

Another volume, of which mention is made—one that is often confused with, but should be distinguished from, the grimoire—is what we may term the Devil's Missal. Probably this had its origin far back in the mist of the centuries among the earliest heretics who passed down their evil traditions to their followers, the Albigenses and the Waldenses or Vaudois.

Enough has been said to show that mischief and malice were part and parcel of the witch's profession, and indeed there was required from them at their reception into this dark society a vow that they would devote themselves wholly to evil. They were moreover pledged to carry on an active Satanist propaganda, to win recruits and to use every endeavour to draw other men and women to their detestable practices and the worship of the fiend. Thus in the case of Janet Breadheid, of Auldearne, we find that her husband " enticed her into that craft ". A girl named Bellot, of Madame Bourignon's academy, confessed that her mother had taken her to the Sabbat when she was quite a child. Another girl alleged that all worshippers of the Devil " are constrained to offer him their children ". At Salem, George Burroughs, a minister, was accused by a large number of women as " the person who had Seduc'd and Compell'd them into the snares of Witchcraft ". Elizabeth Francis, of Chelmsford, a witch tried in 1566, was only about twelve years old when her grandmother taught her the art of sorcery. The Pendle beldame, Mother Demdike, " brought up her owne Children, instructed her Graund-children, and tooke great care and paines to bring them to be Witches." It is hardly to be believed that a modern writer of a certain school—fortunately at once negligible and freakish—should characterize this dedication of young children to hell and the lord of hell as " a ceremony, at once simple and touching ".

To-day the Satanists are thoroughly imbued with the missionary spirit, and are ever eager to enlarge their ranks to the destruction of immortal souls. A very general method is for the Satanist to lure his intended proselyte into the most odious debaucheries, even to tempt him to the commission of some crime, and then if he seem laggard to subscribe his service to the demon and join the infernal gang the pressure of blackmail can be brought to bear until the poor wretch is wholly ensnared and lost. Any defection from the ranks, any attempted betrayal, or in many cases, lukewarmness even, is punished by death. Thus the members are terrorized, and many an unexplained, undiscovered murder is in truth the work of Satanists, the vengeance they have wreaked upon some traitor.

It is not necessary to do more than mention in passing the immense sums of money which have been so lavishly poured out by this dark brotherhood to corrupt and destroy whole countries and nations by their anarchy and red revolutions.

It is a commonplace of Catholic teaching that there has been a True Religion in the world ever since the creation of man—" the Universal Church began with Abel the Just "—and when Christ Himself came this existent True Religion received the designation of Christianity. Opposed to the True Religion throughout was the cult of evil, Satanism.

Witchcraft was potent—indeed more potent than ever after—and the devil had his worshippers before the coming of Christ. Not to speak of the Oriental magic of the Egyptians and the Chaldæans; nor of Hebrew necromancies, which the Bible condemns again and again; sorcerers flourished in Greece and Rome, and the whole body of ancient legislation clearly shows that before the dawn of Christianity, in the paynim era when a multiplicity of heathen cults prevailed throughout the Roman empire, witchcraft was as uncompromisingly prohibited as ever it was denounced and punished by the great Pontiffs, by Innocent VIII and Sixtus V; in Germany during the sixteenth and seventeenth centuries; in England by the parliaments of Elizabeth and James.

It is an empty and utterly baseless theory to suppose (as a certain type of imaginative writer has been indiscreet enough to assert) that witchcraft is the survival of some primitive cult of which nothing is known, concerning which nothing can be definitely discovered, and which is certainly not mentioned in any record or by any author. The development of such a fantasy merely leads to a wholesale wresting of historical facts, to a ludicrous perversion of evidence —probably quite unconsciously misread—and to general cheap claptrap all round.

None of the earlier religions existed with the express design and end of perpetrating evil for evil's sake. Now this constitutes the very essence of witchcraft, which is first and foremost the cult of hell. It is surely permissible to express surprise when one finds Satanism described as " a joyous religion ".

Bit with the novelty of the thing, some enterprising folklorist next asks us to look upon witchcraft " in the light of a fertility cult ", being careful, of course, for convenience sake to ignore the occult phenomena lest the issue be confused. It seems superfluous to remark that not a tittle of sound evidence can be brought forward to support such a *capriccio*.

That here and there lingered various old harmless customs and rustic festivities which had come down from pre-Christian times and which the Church had allowed, nay, had even sanctified by directing them to their right source, the Maypole dances, for example, and the Midsummer fires, which now honour St. John Baptist, is a matter of common knowledge. But there is no continuance of a pagan fertility cult.

Nor will anyone seek to argue from some extraordinary but isolated and infrequent instances of survival. In Easter week, 1282, John, the parish priest of Inverkeithing, celebrated the profane rites of Priapus, collecting young girls from the villages and compelling them to tread a measure in honour of Father Bacchus. When he had led these females forth in a troop, out of sheer wantonness he danced before carrying in front on a pole a representation of the human organs of reproduction, and singing and capering himself like a mime he viewed them all, and stirred them to lust by filthy language. The older men who being scandalized by this shameless performance rebuked him gently because they respected the dignity of his office, he violently abused, and comported himself more madly than ever. He also at dawn in Penance Week insisted that some should prick others who were stripped for penance with sharp goads, and when the graver burgesses protested he sturdily defended these indecencies. One night he was stabbed to death, nor was his assailant discovered.

About a dozen years before these pranks at Inverkeithing a cattle plague had broken out in various districts, which led to the revival of long dead mummeries. Two or three monks, it is said, advised the country folk to erect an image or terminal to Priapus, and through some ritual which involved the lighting of new fire by the friction of wood they prophesied the beasts would be relieved. At Fenton a Cistercian lay-brother actually set up this figure before the hall hearth and sprinkled the byres of the lord of the manor with holy water to which he had added " filthy matters of his own invention ". Here we have an example of a lewd and degraded superstition no doubt, but to talk of " Priapus-worship " and to describe the Cistercians as " monastic wizards " is not a trifle ridiculous, and betrays an extraordinary confusion of ideas.

In 1749 Girolamo Tartarotti (1702-1761), a minor journalist, one of the many literary *abbati* who swarmed throughout Italy at that time writing with equal elegance facile verse and fluent prose, published at Venice a large quarto volume, which he entitled *A Study of the Midnight Sabbats of Witches (Del Congresso Notturno delle Lammie)*. His chapters are composed with an immense parade of learning—he quotes from more than three hundred and eighty authors—perhaps no such wonderful task in those days of leisure and large libraries. He shows himself, as the fashion went, a complete sceptic, and the thesis of this " member of the Republic of Letters ", for so he floridly dubs himself, is that there were never any assemblies or rendezvous of Satanists, and indeed summing it up in a few words that witchcraft is imaginary and a sick dream. *A Study of the Midnight Sabbats of Witches* is a very rare book, Tartarotti has been completely forgotten, and he would not be worth mentioning here were it not for one curious and interesting point. In the course of his excogitations he discusses the famous " Canon Episcopi ", an enactment to be considered in detail later, which speaks of certain women who seduced by the snare of the demon "believe and declare that they ride upon beasts with Diana, goddess of the pagans", and with multitudes of women flying through the air in service and attendance upon her. From this Tartarotti evoked the fantastic idea of a "Dianic cult", and he contends that witchcraft was nothing else than this imaginary cult. (Chapter IX : *The identity of the Dianic Cult with modern witchcraft is demonstrated and proven.*) Actually his arguments, if we may dignify unsupported statements and romancing by this name, could convince nobody, and the whole thing fell to the ground and was ignored.

A recent writer chancing upon Tartarotti's book (either, I suppose, at the British Museum or drawing from the notice in the Soldan-Heppe *Geschichte der Hexenprozesse*) promptly borrowed the idea, and came out with a new thesis concerning "the Dianic cult", "as I propose to call it," which embraced "the religious beliefs and ritual of the people known in late mediæval times as 'Witches'". Of course Tartarotti was never so much as mentioned. The theory was at first mightily commended in certain quarters for its novelty, its scientific modernity, but when in the Foreword to a translation of Remy's *Demonolatry* (1930) I happened to show that Tartarotti's crochet had long since been discredited and had fallen into oblivion, the "Dianic cult" was speedily dropped, and very little (I believe) has since been heard of it.

Witchcraft does not belong to the antiquarian past ; it lives and energizes, a monstrous and fearful menace to-day, and it is perhaps only by a clear and understanding view of the history of black magic that we can be aware of the imminent dangers which surround us.

As the Duke of Lauderdale once wrote: " It is impertinent arguing to conclude, that because there have been Cheats in the World, because there are some too credulous, and some have been put to Death for Witches, and were not, therefore all Men are deceived."

www.ingramcontent.com/pod-product-compliance
Lightning Source LLC
Chambersburg PA
CBHW022111160426
43198CB00028B/719